Make Space

poems

J. A. Lagana

Finishing Line Press
Georgetown, Kentucky

Make Space

Copyright © 2023 by J. A. Lagana
ISBN 979-8-88838-226-4 First Edition
All rights reserved under International and Pan-American Copyright Conventions. No part of this book may be reproduced in any manner whatsoever without written permission from the publisher, except in the case of brief quotations embodied in critical articles and reviews.

Publisher: Leah Huete de Maines
Editor: Christen Kincaid
Cover Art: Vincent Hawley, "Bridge View"
Author Photo: Tony Lagana
Cover Design: Elizabeth Maines McCleavy

Order online: www.finishinglinepress.com
also available on amazon.com

Author inquiries and mail orders:
Finishing Line Press
P. O. Box 1626
Georgetown, Kentucky 40324
U. S. A.

Table of Contents

I.

What grief said 1
Letter to Stephen Regarding That Night in April 2
She Laughed Like a School Girl 4
Heart Failure and the Sugars 5
During the season she was dying 6
One day we moved her toward the kitchen 7
How to be a Tomato 8
Between Sisters 9
On Sharing Carvel with Aunt Roneta 10
Driving I-95 South While the Tiger Lilies Are in Bloom ... 12
Driving River Road in April 13
Regarding Matthew 14
Afterwards, walking 15
What grief said 16

II

What grief said 19
After Lunch in Some Seaside Town 20
How Anxiety Interferes 21
The Clearing 22
She Favored the Scent of Fabergé's Aphrodisia 23
Near the End of Things My Sister and I Visit Our Father .. 24
Two Photographs, One Recent 25
After the New Age Fair 27
Pulled from his bureau's top drawer and all a glimmer 28
Along Fleecy Dale Road and in Conversation with Myself ... 29
What grief said 31

III

What grief said 35
At the kitchen table, maybe in the afternoon 36
Since the tow path offers the quickest route to the river ... 37

Everyone Gathered As We Were Back Then 38
Regarding that Photograph 39
Our Son Has Unexpectedly Returned Home 40
Our Son Sits in That Old Arm Chair 41
Two Sisters in Cashmere and Capris 42
On occasion I'll spray Aphrodisia with abandon 43
There is a Mermaid in Aisle Seven 44
Reverie After Time Spent Alone 45
Even though I will eventually tire 46
What grief said 47

Acknowledgements 48
About the author 51

For
Alfred & Alfreda

I

What grief said

Conduct a sweep.

           Use a broom with bristles so stiff

your floors will scar.   Gather up wayward strands

of hair and thread and seaglass. Clear the dust

        from every photograph. Add river stones.

Add bits of prayer and paper.

                          Wrap the remnants in satin

or a favorite scarf.
                Rid yourself of all and any clutter.

The dead will understand.

Letter to Stephen Regarding That Night in April

I thought you were asleep, although the only time anyone
ever slept on the landing was that night Charlie came home

drunk from an office party, *too many sheets to the wind,*
you said. So, it wasn't odd to see you there, on the landing,

stretched out, a sheet up to your neck. Your arms, extended
as if you were waiting for me to grasp your hand

and lead you in another direction. The way the medics
tended to you, the reflecting blue and red lights

caught in the hallway mirrors. You would have liked the almost
dance hall mood to everything. Time was out of sorts,

so it wasn't odd that the floors seemed fluid. The stair railings,
as I remember, rattled and swerved as if

the earth were tremoring. The stars, glimpsed
through the upper foyer window, (I think I was running),

were too high to be taken seriously.
Each carpeted step must have sprung wildflowers

with thick patches of puffed grey orbs
like the ones we pulled from the yard

when we were kids. I could never seem
to move as quickly as I wanted through them either.

Make a wish, one of us would say, each of us
holding on too tightly to a bunch of skinny, wilted stems

you had readied for the ceremonious exhaling of our breaths.
Even, forced exhales, so deep, that the dandelion seeds sprayed

outward in a rush, fanning over the lawn, like splatter spit,
nearly guaranteeing new growth the following spring.

My wish, mumbled and sincere, would be for something silly,
like *make Jamie Rogers fall in love with me.*

Only on the landing that night the world turned serious.
I wished only for you to stay.

I don't recall who else was there,
just their voices, anxious and low.

A car may have passed by, someone outside was maybe talking
to their dog, there might have been a plane flying overhead

and the birds were starting up again. Earlier, you were brushing your teeth,
we'd been talking about how the history of things

is not always what actually happened. There was the sound
of faucet water pulsing through the house, the pipes thumping

as the water worked its way upward, eventually hitting
the cold stone sink, the thud of the cabinet door after you'd rummaged

through for floss or nail clippers and maybe that bottle of pills.
The calling of the night as good. Good night, *Good night.* Later, a commotion.

Stumbling and shouts. Your body, lifeless. Your breath, somewhere else.
Afterwards, an imprint. The mark of the ambulance stretcher

on the landing's thick green carpet. Two deep and evenly lined
impressions that we could never vacuum out.

That house is long gone. Some days,
I am still kneeling on the landing, pleading with you.

She Laughed Like a School Girl

The way my mother liked orderly things.
Her potted geraniums,   grouped by color.
   Her boxwoods,   edging the patio.
   Her whispers of praise,   reserved.

The way her fingers tapped
       her collarbone to readjust
       the glistening strands that fell
            in measured scallops across her chest
            like a rising sun that only she could see.

Heart Failure and the Sugars

i.
One night she said, *Here, here, come sit here,*
I'll make space for you, but I was in a hurry
you know how it was, the commute
and grad school calling too, and
I said *sure, sure, I'll be right up,* but
I can't say that I was, on that night,
any kind of present.

ii.
One afternoon she cried, *Oh, oh, oh,*
as if she were singing backup,
her hands and body swaying in time
to a breathless tempo. Did she sense me
in the hallway, trying to redirect
her body,   which had turned heavy and lost?
She missed the bedroom door,
          made a left instead,
straight into the hallway wall.
          She resisted the teenage me,
as if she were crazy drunk.
                    Her feet,
          one in front of the other,
                    shuffling on the green carpeting.
Her forehead thump- thump- thumping into that wall—
until the ambulance arrived.   She was in a heap by then.
Her face, purpling.

iii.
What kind of a life is this? She'd ask on nights
made worse by growing isolation. A daily *Diet Pepsi*
her single pleasure, forsaken.   Her energies,
depleted,   her svelte figure,   gone.   Once,
she had showgirl's legs,
could outdance her sister or anyone else
game enough.
                              Turn that music up, she'd say.

During the season she was dying

                we'd dab her neck and wrists
                with her favorite musky floral scent
until it assailed
                the stagnant smells of illness
        that permeated the house
        which grew tired
        from facing those bitter seasons
                          while she lay dreaming
        in the front room   quietly taking leave.

What of the contrast between the striking softness in her eyes
        and her face, so swollen then,
so dull and grey like river stones, worn
        by the steady push of water and sun? *Too much of any good thing*
won't amount to much, she'd say, adding a *"tsch, tsch"*
in case we didn't understand.

                      Morning wind-lashed windows,
wretched cold filled the cracks between the panes
                where hope once rested
                    in our best plans to keep her pain at bay.

                In the hallway, regrets.

        Low and in a cloudless sky,
        a white crescent moon.

One day we moved her toward the kitchen

where she side-glanced out the window
and sipped a chocolate milkshake,
amused.
        The sun's shine spilling
across the linoleum floor.
It was days before her death.

                Against the back fence,
a line of lush forsythia,
their yellow branches
lively, blooming wildly.

How to be a Tomato

Watch for earthworms
working root-tangled soil,
notice other omens. The low
setting sun; the crows flying east,
the shadows on fields resting
under an otherwise Utah-blue sky,
the quick evening breeze pulling at you,
the nestling leaves, the calming
scents of earth and border rock.
Don't regret what's gone. Anticipate
the prick of the paring knife. Trust
that it will come and when it does,
hope the blade will catch. Hope
that it will tear away the bruised
and tender marks that come
from sitting in the sun too long
from being picked
at by beetles, from having
thin skin, from falling
among rocks. Imagine
that the pulp
around the deepest scars
is sweetest.

Between Sisters

In Greek mythology, the Neikea or Neikos were the spirits of arguments and quarrels, born of Eris, the Goddess of Discontent.

Grudges so deep
no one remembers
how they first took root,
turned wild, thrived in anger.

Quarrels as unpredictable as wild marsh marigolds caught up in wood grass.

Oh, white lies and anger.
   The Neikos, skirting around
     while you borrowed
       one another's dresses and fought
         for center stage. Resentments stashed
      in hatboxes, lined up in rows of patent leather shoes,
   buried in purses paired with pearl drop earrings.

   The *Neikos* studying
     one of you sipping lemon tea
     from vintage china, the other drinking Diet Pepsi
       from crystal. Both of you, angst-filled—
    your children and their children's children
   paying the price for every fight.

Oh, harsh words.
   Not everything flourishes in tough conditions.

On Sharing Carvel with Aunt Roneta

Toes crunching sand, we sit snugly
in our beach chairs, bound by faded
cool aluminum, twenty years
between us,
red webbing scratches our skin,
our legs lift and stretch
and smack the waves.

I am banana-chocolate swirl,
packed tightly in a sugar cone.
She is crushed
walnuts, crumbs surfing down the side
of "Good Green" pistachio.

She is thirty-six, not yet the mother
of the son
who will leave one day in anger,
hurling words down gray papered hallways.

>She has not been hurt yet
>by the husband who will wrap his hands
>around her throat,
>straddle her, and slam her head
>against their couch's wooden arm
>one late August Sunday night
>back home in Jersey City.

>Then her eyes will blacken,
>her neck and face will burst with color,
>her shoulders, a palette of green, will bear blue
>fingerprint impressions,
>her lips will pour red.

She is glorious,
melting slowly.

We will walk the boards tonight, laughing,
eyeing boys in purple plaid Bermudas,

their tan legs pumping pedals,
heading towards Asbury Park.

Breathing in the taffy scents.
Breathing in the sea air.

Driving I-95 South While the Tiger Lilies Are In Bloom

There's the urge to tailgate
        a rusted 18-wheeler.
The forward
        and away pace of traffic
moves us through what weighs heavily anyway.
                Your subdued funeral, all of us undone.
No sign of your sister.
The director told us,
        She slipped in mid-service
      sat by herself   in the last row.
Snuck into the wake   after hours the day before.
Stood alone.

            What was it with you two?
            You always said she was never one
for gatherings or for anything
where she wasn't   the main draw.

The organist's vocal rendition of *Ava Maria*
                    would have made you cringe.
The rest of us teared up solemnly, gathered afterwards for wine and dinner.
No one danced, but the old favs kept playing.

The fumes from the truck ahead,
   circle back,
      fade like a last breath.
         This morning, the highway—
                fringed with lilies.

Driving River Road in April

It is after all, a rough time.
Muck and mud. Forsythia raging.
Frigid sky for miles. Every hint of green
that pushes through undauntedly
will flourish with the certainty
of brighter days ahead.
Behold as small deaths give way.
Bittercress   crocus   blue phlox
forcibly breaking ground, reestablishing
their rightful places
        in the strewn thawing acres
of fields nearly overcome
by last season's remnants. The ground
steadying for more to come.

Regarding Matthew

He bore our family's traits,
        stubbornness,
and eyes as grey as the Atlantic in December.
        Spare me your half-hearted compliments,
he'd shout toward his tight-lipped mother, who left trails
of Final Net   and disappointment,   who sat drenched
in dark sweaters with Kleenex-stuffed sleeves.
        Don't you see me? he'd cry, toward the shadows
of a father who left
        blue fingerprint impressions.

        Beyond the father's reach,   drawn toward roiling waves,
weighted down by flashbacks, harsh words,
cold recollections of straps that still stung.   Unexpected slaps,
the lingering fade of bruises. The tides crackling.
        His mind, stuck in a starless midnight.
In his ears, the roar of beach house pinks and grays.
In his mouth the taste of grit, sea glass.
Sand prints   hiss behind him.

There was a wispy tattooed love
who offered humor and pointed toward
life's sunnier side.   *Stop*
    with the half-hearted compliments,
he'd say, his words bursting like fireworks floating
        over darkened waters.
        Don't you see me?

            Come spring, he ditched his pills,
walked into a rush
        of cracked mussel shells and tide
        until the ocean overtook him. His body, found
along a beach and eventually.
        All compliments are meaningless,
he once told me. *They're half-hearted,*
empty. Jesus, please, he said, *spare me.*

Afterwards, walking

it hurt to look ahead.　There was that sinking
feeling of catastrophe and change. Cross-tipped
shadows　　　　　wild reeds rising
from the edges of the muddied　　　pond.
　　　Ragged light　dank earth　　agitated bullfrogs.
A repeated rush　　　of nerves　　doubt.
The winds picking up.　　　The way
endings come on suddenly,
　　　　the downpour that follows.

What grief said

I'm not as powerful
as water and wind.   Those two
                      will rip up shore towns
                              wreck anything
                                    vibrant along a river.

II

What grief said

That was you, yes?

        Weeping with the music turned up?

        The windows rolled tight. The low tides and clouds.
The highway's boring stretch.   Diminished traffic.

    The calmness afterwards.

                                            Yes, yes.

After Lunch in Some Seaside Town

We raged brilliant that October afternoon.
Colored cords and silver round our wrists,
aromas of sweet corn, cumin. The salted air.

A row of blackbirds balanced tentatively
on high tension wires. The boardwalk,
nearly empty. Subdued tides reclaimed shells
and beaten strands of seaweed as if determined
to obscure what lay broken.

We rarely understood what the other was thinking,
although we recognized what was easy, the tempos of the waters,
the old family stories, how closely our faces
resembled one another.

Who at the table could predict
your death come spring?

You, a flicker, like a bright speck
from a disappearing sun. A faded
hue atop wrinkled waters.

When that day drifts back, I wonder,
would you have remembered
how the sky opened?

The way the ocean's pulse
slowed? How the rain
wouldn't quit?

How Anxiety Interferes

It urges you
to rip up
every photo of the dead so that
you are really done with them. It argues
that longing is a waste of time. It plays
with your breathing, nags you
to bury the kitchen table, to start throwing
pieces of silverware into the Delaware
once the Pink Moon rises. It demands
you make an offering for every moment
that didn't turn into what you had hoped. Later,
it becomes about fear. Of losing your teeth,
your breath, your way. Go, drive
with the windows down
over the toll bridge.

Listen
for the chime of river water
moving through ice.

Worry
won't let you see that everything
moves forward—but, it does,
like geese flying somberly
at dawn,
through an inevitable
and gradually
brightening sky.

The Clearing

                The rocking chairs sold,
        veiled in sea salt
            and the ghosts of the sisters—
our mothers, who, we were sure
still lingered on the front porch,
      silent, angry, yet charmed
          by the ocean across the way.
         There was the pile of stuff
     we hauled to the curb,
rusted pans, mirrors where the silver ran old,
      pockmarked boogie boards,
arm chair cushions.
         We lodged brass stops
and sea rocks to keep the front and back doors
     from slamming.   The screens
         grayed thin, bowed from decades
of salt air and regrets
      as bitterns,
          gulls, egrets and herons clamored
amid strands of what hadn't sold
     or couldn't be cast aside.
      There were the old mayo jars
we carried to the beach filled
     with ice-cubes and tea when we hadn't any cares
but to ride waves and shift our beach umbrellas
        while the sun's shadows
    tracked time.   A neighbor took the lamp
with the shell-filled base. The crucifix
    that hung above the kitchen stove
was wrapped in a plaid shirt and buried
     in the yard.   We cleared shells from the shelves,
whelks, moon snails, jingles, razor clams,
    lifted some to our ears, got lost in the echoes,
felt the breezes shift.
       Ah, we said, as the cacophonies
     ran silent.   The old place   now,
     in repose,   full of light.

She Favored the Scent of Fabergé's Aphrodisia

Still and semi-filled
            with that mossy-colored
unforgettable scent. I kept three,
        each capped
                in speckled gold, an orderly
        nudged lineup on the back corner
of my bureau.   The levels evaporate
        slightly each year. After decades,
        my mother's perfume bottles remain
        half-full.
                Time, if what they say
        is true, you'll dilute our losses—
                        diminish our longing
        for what's wafted away.

Near the End of Things My Sister and I Visit Our Father

           My sister looks towards me like I've got answers.
She paces the red floral rug.
Its frayed edges make me anxious.
Sparks fly, but our father stares ahead,
indifferent
           to a favored *Bougarabou* drum,
           a sculpture of a blue cat,
           some photos of the dead,
           our mother, his brothers, the dog.
Eventually the night sky darkens.

He's golden in the lamplight now,
All other furies stay forgotten,
lost in once familiar rooms.
           These hallways seem much narrower now,
           he tells her. He thinks they met at a coffee shop
           in Philly back in 1997, but can't be sure.
           She looks familiar, he says.
I think I know you.
To me, he says, *You worked at the station.*

He walks rigidly
past a tea-stained couch,
trips over a streak of moonlight,
           reaches toward the ceiling,
           as if there is a rope
           to hold on to,
           rises shakily,
as if grabbing fistfuls of stars.

He jams them deep into his pockets,
recalls later,
how their acidic smoking startled him,
how the pinch of glowing hot ash stung.

Two Photographs, One Recent

In this one,
I am twenty-something,
holding a large bluefish and smiling.
Tan, fit, beautiful really—even though my mother
has been dead for nearly three months.
I am on a charter boat
off the coast of New Jersey
in the middle of the Atlantic
in the middle of July,
smiling for the camera my father holds,
while the ocean
crashes all around us.

In this one,
I'm holding a little boy and a pumpkin.
It is a bright Saturday and the boy
is my son and we have just drunk
paper cupfuls of cider and have been
on a hayride and still,
there is a corn maze to visit.
The wind and his arms wrap tightly
around me. I am newly forty.
My husband snaps another shot
then tells me I look beautiful, even though
my father has been dead since Monday.
That night, I cupped my father's face
as he drifted in a morphine haze.
As he died, I kissed his forehead
and may have mumbled
something like *how I have loved you.*
His cheeks, still warm.
I kept looking at the ceiling
as if he were up there
watching.

In the pumpkin field
the sky, never bluer.

A rustle of cornstalks
signals another winter.

After the New Age Fair

It is nearly midnight when I walk out on my back porch
to place agate topaz moonstone along the wooden deck railing

at just the right angles like the woman at the New Age fair suggested.
I think about the healers there, who read my aura, massaged my hands,

and predicted what life had in store. I had my cards read by Steve
who scanned my palms and saw my energy as bad. His rings of garnet,

garish. He offered to burn candles, one a day,
every day, for seven weeks to dispel such bad energy.

He wore heavy stones of topaz in his ears. Brown stones, reminding me
of my mother. How she and I would stand together at the kitchen sink

washing dirt off fresh potatoes, their dark skins pulled tightly round
the sweet cool flesh we knew was waiting underneath. Our hands

would smooth away each fleck of dirt as water from the faucet
trickled down like the Erie Street lamp light pouring through

her bedroom blinds on that night when I was kneeling
at her bedside, in my father's place, soothing her pained, bloated feet

in a pan of cool clear water. She was crying and I was careful
not to further irritate the splitting skin around her ankles at her heels

between her toes any further than the fluid buildup had done by now.
My fingers moved slowly as her feet shimmered

swollen in the water, catching light. How could we
have known her death would come so soon?

Pulled from his bureau's top drawer and all a glimmer

my father's collection of rosary beads—gathered over
the decades from his years in the war, from marriages,
baptisms, some deaths, and then others. Nearly the entire family,
represented in the lidded crystal jar filled with flimsy silver chains,
a glisten of beads, brown, white, cylindrical. Pinkish
specks and intertwined crucifixes, a loose dozen
sending red and blue glints bouncing off the jar's rim
like the glow around the planet I watched
from the hallway's windows before dawn today,
merely hours   after   his death   waiting, waiting.
Isn't it amazing how much is visible
to the naked eye in such deep darkness?
I wasn't thinking about mourning—
only watching the planet. It was either Saturn or Mars,
I'm never really certain, only mesmerized, seeing it
caught up in its own pulsing atmosphere. Its offering
of blue, red, and white light
issuing forth like a deep space blessing.

Along Fleecy Dale Road and in Conversation with Myself

healing (n.)
"from heal (v) Old English hælan "cure; save; make whole...and well,"

i.
The next hill comes quickly.
The river, always on the right.　　　　*Not quite the River Lethe, no use*
　　　　　　　　　　　　　　　　　　　in forgetting　　everyone.

Farmhouses,　barns.　　　　　　　　　*The first painted red*
Remnants.　　　　　　　　　　　　　　*a mix of rust,　dirt,　paint.*

ii.
A curve of corn fields,
knee-high by the Fourth of July.　　　*You know that's just a saying, right?*

There are deer　　waiting.　　　　　　*Watch the road.*
There's not much to be done about timing.　　*A few ghosts, echoing, still.*

iii.
What is it with the dead?　　　　　　　*They won't leave well enough alone.*

They know their anniversaries.
　　　They know to stop by　　　　　　*They come back as remnants.*
just when you've been able to sleep
　　　through the night again,
or are finally noticing the horses grazing.　　*Perfect as posted pictures.*
Stone bridges, wooden fences,
　　　field grasses.　　　　　　　　　　*Momentarily present.*

iv.
Everything passes.　　　　　　　　　　*Well, technically, yes.*

v.
In the highest branches,
turkey vultures, leaning in together,　*As if in conversation.*
shaking out their feathers.

A few hunched along the ledge
of a farmhouse roof.

*Either a sign of death
or a sign of healing.*

What grief said

You always liked that lilac tree.
The wizened one
that flourished
near the forsythia.
      How its cut blossoms
scented your room.
      Late night laughter
trickling in through the screens.

          Most days grace is everywhere
in this dreamscape
called your life.
        There are strains of fiddles
          in the distance
a formation of geese overhead
      everything in rhythm.   Yes. Yes.
   You'll come to accept
that nearly everyone
      you've ever loved is dead.

              You'll think you see them
          in passing, the runner by the pond,
       the lady on the Avenue, the gentleman
     moving past you at the grocery store.
         You'll search everywhere for signs,
           feel sure the blackbirds resting
     on the water tower when you walk by,
      or that sporty two-door—driving
      a usually empty road—are messages
           for you. That song again,
              twice on the radio.

III

What grief said

      You can't afford
to spend all of your time with me.

                    You'll miss everything.

                    You'll never be
                              a mother's daughter,
                  a father's favorite,
                  a sister,
                          or the close one
                  again.

      You'll be other things.

At the kitchen table, maybe in the afternoon

I tell my mother
I am pregnant
and she says
oh, isn't that wonderful
and smiles
then says
there is much to be done
and I imagine
all we'll do together
in preparation
for this first child
we are all
thrilled to welcome
except the chair
where my mother sits
in this dream
and the wrap dress
she is wearing
are not
recognizable.
The table
between us,
wider than
the decades since her death.
She glances
my way momentarily
as if I am vaguely familiar.

Since the tow path offers the quickest route to the river

we slip down rocks
and dirt, holding on to ragged branches and one another for
support, it's December, the morning sun's so low everything
else seems dreary—we head out to the center of the wing
dam rising from rippling waters, you tread confidently ahead,
balancing us along the dam's edge, ignoring the cluster of gulls
who are full of complaints and every shade of grey. I'm more
unsure of the snapping winds despite a sense that my balance is
ok, that we are not likely to fall. There's little river town weekend
traffic, the tourists kept away by the early hour and the rawness
of the day. L'ville Bridge is as steadying a sight as I've ever seen.
I keep my sights set ahead and on you. The wind challenges us
to step together, to stay steady. The gulls cackle-loop and there's
relief when you grab my hand. I'm awed by the sliced sunlight-
tipped eddies and all that seems possible today.

Everyone Gathered As We Were Back Then

No one worn from too many disappointments or from hours commuting up and down the Interstate. No one angry or dead. My father, sitting at the head of the table. My mother, wearing her pearls and fussing over the macaroni salad as her sister lets the gravy run cool before placing it near the potatoes.

Do you see how it was once the dishes were cleared? Stephen, rolling his sleeves, Matthew, donning rubber gloves before washing the china. He'll sip a second cherry soda with a double splash of Seagram's.

Go, sit with the girls. Learn to roll dice and play sevens and pinochle. You'll laugh at their stories of dates with smooth talkers who lived off Pavonia Avenue. My father has tales about San Francisco after the war. Let the dessert be a strawberry shortcake brought straight from that bakery right off Journal Square. Let our son dance like he's got nothing to lose.

Let him jump from the green-carpeted living room stairs to the landing below with sheer glee at the sight of us all—whirling to polkas and the beats of the Bossa Nova. Let our boy be too wiped out to witness Grandma Maggie touching up her bright red lips before her ten-p.m. ride with aunts and cousins and grandfather in tow, back up the Jersey Turnpike and over the Pulaski Skyway. Her Titanesque mouth a passing visual highlight for the toll collectors at Exit 15E.

Listen for my mother's tone of proud, restrained, approval.

Regarding that Photograph

The one that made the papers—
our son, so assured,
                      swagged in graduation silks and tassels.
(His father can't stop smiling.)
      I long to send *that* photograph to you,
but the house on Erie sold years ago,
      your numbers, long disconnected.
No working email or social media can reach you.
              Yet, in the atmosphere's static-filled silences
there remains a glistening of you
              within the core of electric currents
      pulsing with ions, vapor,
        argon,   nitrogen,   drifting   north, southeast, west,
                over and around this planet,
the essence of who and what   you once were,
                my mother, my father,
   floating by in minute particles.   Privy to what came before
and all that may   perhaps,   follow.

Our Son Has Unexpectedly Returned Home

We mix black cardamom with red chili paste,
dice dates, sear mushroom stems and fruit,
watch them crinkle, go golden.

Bowls of gingered rice wait in repose.
How patient we've become. It's been weeks
since he's returned.   There is no other place to go,
so we focus on this meal, our collaborative success.

I grate. He peels. He plates. I garnish.

Everything, flavorable, scented. Vibrant
like the pictures, scarves, and texts he'd send
from the other place he loved.

After dinner, his bedroom's
open door allows a glimpse
      of rowed boxes on his laptop screen,
        a zoom of faces with voices I'm not privy to—
          books and papers strewn about his feet
like dust from the Buenos Aires streets he strolled
      a month or so ago.
          Those sights and scents must pull and linger.
He seldom speaks of sun-worn storefront awnings,
     the daily mingle of passersby, the whiffs of yerba mate,
 of scrolled headlines not yet full
     of canceled flights,
         or the dread of sickness seeping forth.
Those mornings, hopeful
     like an easy reverie
where time is plentiful.

                                 -April 2020

Our Son Sitting in That Old Arm Chair

If he knows I'm watching, he doesn't let on and runs his hands along the cat's long-haired gray body. The two of them, silent, one with closing eyes, the other, staring straight ahead, possibly contemplating a next move.

-June 2020

Two Sisters in Cashmere and Capris

Sunday afternoons are when I miss them most.
That's when I'll catch myself
rewashing the roasting pans
while staring out the window. I'll catch a glimpse
of one of them, her lime green sleeves
peeking out from behind the dogwood; the other one laughing
in the branches of the plum tree.
Her patent leather pumps and matching bag
catch an edge of afternoon light as she points
towards the tulips. Their scents of *Final Net*
and Fabergé's *Aphrodisia* hang heavily in the air.
The flavors from Eris' fruits of discord
not evident
in their squinting smiles
or linked arms.

Sometimes they wave
and say, *Come here and stand alongside the hydrangea*
where the air is thick and sweet.
That's when I'll realize
the television is on
or that I probably need a drink.

In an upstairs hallway photograph
they are forever leaning
up against a fading front porch rail, the ocean angled in
behind them. The dog and I may see them later—
dancing in the reflections of the downtown storefront windows.
The Twist, the Polka—the Polonaise was always their favorite.

Yesterday, under a smooth sky
of clipped moon and constellations,
the dog caught their scents and barked.
                We were headed toward the river
and kept walking.

On occasion I'll spray Aphrodisia with abandon

inhaling the fragranced air
                as if my past and future selves
depend upon the slow inhalation of my mother's vintage scent
and the repeated whispering of her name. This ceremonious
reenactment, a reconnection, an incantation from memory,
                how both of us were, at one time,
breathing in the same rooms
together.

There is a Mermaid in Aisle Seven

> After John William Waterhouse's, *A Mermaid* (1900)

That red-clay look in your eyes.
How do you tell, if it's dusk or dawn?
Some days, I can't be sure.
Diminished beauty
waiting in a tepid tidal pool,
combed ringlets skim clear
while I seek out a box of kosher salt
from the lower shelves. Bored
and bedazzled, you're half-naked,
on an iron-on tee shirt--
worn by someone searching
for oregano.   Your scales, detailed.
Your argent fin, those pearls, dulled
under faded stars. That shirt hangs with age
and you look disappointed. I'm here
for solace as if some buried treasure awaits
among quick bread mixes and spice.
I'll skim my phone for what it is I think I need.
         You've skimmed light-drenched waters.
Now, we're both caught in this current
of strangers, this jangle of carts. Jars of honey
and mustard roll, rattle, catch bits of light
like sea anemones visible in lower tides,
with little claim to hallowed space. Beyond
a row of checkout lines,
this day spills forth. How will it go?
From here? I can't be sure.

Reverie After Time Spent Alone

Each day scrapes against another.   There is fear
of losing pace & place.   How effortlessly
dawn streams   from midnight.
Twice today   I danced   alone   trusting
the music   to carry me. Finger snaps & slow jazz rising,
the kitchen's wavy window glass   cadenced.
      I should have been doing the dishes.

The sky   all cloudscape anymore.
    The ocean's call   loud & far.
    Each of us centered   in our ways.
I worry less   about what can't be changed.

There is a garter snake   resting   in the boxwood's upper branches.
      Ocean waves   against
indifferent boulders.   Are there blackbirds   waiting
   on the water tower?

Let's stand & watch the full & fabulous   orange moon
    rise   over our hills month by month   such stillness.
    We'll walk   curved roads   side-streets
     up & down   & up again   through crunched snow
or with newly fallen leaves underfoot,
    our breathes rising   translucent.
River mist   across the way on any given morning.
   There are days when the sky seems enough.
 I wonder   if my ghosts still watch.

As these winds shift   will we   gather again?
The lawn chairs are waiting   as is our favorite wine.

     What time shall we walk today?
        Which way shall we go?

Even though I will eventually tire

of putting one step in front of the other
and heading out,
        along the sidewalks and cross-streets
                along roads that curve
                      and lead down one way
and up another,
    I can't get enough of the
            grey sky
                    or the undercoat spread of branch-brown grasses
or how beautiful
leaves look, their veined backs burnished
        against asphalt.
               Downed branches,
                    like sculptures, twigs, cast in dirt, muddied and random.
I can't get over
how beautiful it is to walk
the same path day after day.

                    Today the pond was frozen.
              The path and fields
     held the same grey from last week's snow.
     There were no birds chattering.
          There was no heron pausing
                at the far edge under the river birches.
                    There were no bullfrogs acting up.

The grey curbstones,
also, beautiful. The eight deer
passing in a line, as true
as everything else.
    One, glanced my way,
held my gaze
        long enough
                long enough
to sense I understood.
                        ...this is what we have been trying
                        to tell you.

Of course, I replied. Yes, of course.

What grief said

Gather every version
of your faded family.
Wrap their memories.
        A favored cloth will do.
Bundle tightly,
the way you would
your first-born's tooth,
his clip of curls.
                      Place these
              precious and compact,
      upon something sweetly scented.
                      Cover with off-handed things—
an unsent card, a dried-out pen,
      gauze and shells, a half-filled notebook page,
a neatly-folded woven shawl sent from somewhere else.
                    Don't close the drawer entirely.

Keep watch like those backyard birds,
      whose brindled feathers blend
against speckled bark.
                    Go, tie ribbons
      round your head
      like a folk tale child
            warning off dread.
                      Sing songs with made up words.
Cast pebbles into the river or along the ocean's edge.

      You'll still dream you are standing in an old family photograph.

      I won't always   interfere.
I promise.   Still, make space.
                      Make space.
                              I know. I know.

Acknowledgements

Many thanks to the editors of the following publications in which current, early, or different versions of these poems have appeared or are forthcoming:

Amethyst Review: "Even though I will eventually tire"

Atlanta Review: "After the New Age Fair" and "How to Be a Tomato"

Burningword Literary Journal: "After Lunch in Some Seaside Town"

Cider Press Review: "Pulled from his bureau's top drawer and all a glimmer"

formercactus: "Two Sisters in Cashmere and Capris"

Hole in the Head Review: "At the kitchen table, maybe in the afternoon"

Hyacinth Review: "Driving River Road in April"

Naugatuck River Review:
"Letter to Stephen, Regarding that Night in April"
"Heart Failure and the Sugars" (Finalist, Naugatuck River Review's 13th Annual Narrative Poetry Contest)
"Near the End of Things, My Sister and I Visit Our Father" (Finalist, Naugatuck River Review's 10th Annual Narrative Poetry Contest)

Paterson Literary Review: "On Sharing Carvel with Aunt Roneta"

POETiCA Review: "How Anxiety Interferes"; "Regarding Matthew"; "Ghosts" (lines from the poem "Ghosts" were absorbed into "What grief said {You always liked that lilac tree}"

Anthology: *A Certain Kind of Swagger* (Eds. M. Kane, L. Kumar, W. Fulton Steginsky): "There is a Mermaid in Aisle Seven"

~ ~ ~

To Tony, my husband, and to Anthony, our son, thank you for your faithful encouragement and love.

To Peter Murphy, whose encouragement broadened my sense of my creative self, thank you. I remain appreciative.

Thank you to the late Dr. Christopher Bursk for his generosity and critical eye.

To Cheryl Soback, my long-time friend and original first reader, thank you for lighting the way down so many creative paths. To Robbin Farr, thank you for your close readings. To members of the *River Heron Review* and Bucks County poetry and writing communities, thank you for your support and friendships. To the New Hope Beat Poets group, especially Roy Wordsmith and Barry Gross, thank you for maintaining a flourishing creative environment, one that, for me, is instrumental.

J. A. Lagana's poetry has appeared in *Atlanta Review, Burningword Literary Journal, Cider Press Review, Heron Tree, Rattle,* and elsewhere. A founder and former co-editor of *River Heron Review*, she lives in the Bucks County, Pennsylvania river town of New Hope with her family and their cat. Learn more about her at jlagana.com.

www.ingramcontent.com/pod-product-compliance
Lightning Source LLC
Chambersburg PA
CBHW020934180426
43192CB00036B/1141